# GHOSTS OF ERIE COUNTY
## ...and Other Strange Tales

by

**Stephanie Wincik**

To my family

# TABLE OF CONTENTS

# INTRODUCTION

Erie County, situated in the upper northwest corner of Pennsylvania, is an area ripe with tales of hauntings, unusual sightings, and other "eerie" events (sorry, but I couldn't resist the pun). Erie County's history alone lends itself well to stories of the supernatural. For example (in a story not for the squeamish), Mad Anthony Wayne, well-known general of the Revolutionary War era, is said to haunt the roads between Erie and Philadelphia on a never-ending quest to reunite his bones with the flesh that was boiled away from them.

If you visit the city of Erie, located on the shores of Presque Isle, you will immediately notice the maritime theme that dominates many of the city's tourist attractions, hotels, and restaurants. It follows, then, that some of Erie's ghost stories would also include a taste of the nautical, from the tale of "Mariner Mike", deceased owner of a well-known bayside eatery who some believe may still be in town, to the well-documented accounts of UFO sightings on a Presque Isle beach.

Western Erie County also boasts its share of ghostly phenomena. An historic covered bridge is the focus of multiple legends, including reports of a female apparition seen hurling an infant into the icy creek beneath the bridge. In rural Girard, a farmhouse that was the site of a double murder in 1933 is now plagued by unexplained happenings. A century-old home in Albion, recently destroyed by a tornado, once housed the ghost of its former owner.

These stories and others came to me in a number of ways. Many were told to me first-hand by the individuals who actually experienced them, a couple were taken from newspaper accounts, and still others are local legends. These legends, although more than likely not based in actual fact, are included here simply because they are so inextricably woven into the fabric of Erie County history that a book such as this would not be complete without them.

Understandably, some individuals interviewed for this book did not wish to have their identities revealed. In these cases, a fictitious name is used and the story is listed as being from an anonymous source at the end of this book.

To those folks who allowed me to use their stories, please let me say "thank you" for trusting me with this most personal information. Too often, accounts of what we believe to be supernatural events are kept hidden from others for fear of ridicule. But who is to say that these experiences are "supernatural", and not just "natural" events that we as human beings do not yet fully understand? Perhaps those people who we doubt or scoff at for reporting paranormal experiences are actually way ahead of the pack, far more in tune with the yet-to-be-discovered forces in the universe than the rest of us.

What *are* ghosts, anyway? Nobody really knows the answer to this question, I suppose, but those who have been studying ghosts and otherwordly phenomena for many years have theorized that what we perceive as

6

ghostly apparitions are most likely psychic impressions left behind by individuals who experienced a sudden, violent death or some other traumatic event near the end of their earthly lives. Since scientists have told us that energy can never be destroyed but merely changes form, and we know that electrical energy powers our bodies, then what happens to this energy when our bodies die? Is it not reasonable to assume that some or all of this energy could be left behind, particularly if the deceased person died so suddenly that he or she cannot grasp what has happened?

I gave some thought to this question several years ago while visiting Gettysburg, Pennsylvania. The first time I drove into this little town where thousands of young men had lost their lives in the Civil War, my watch stopped. Coincidence? Probably. Still, I couldn't help thinking about the enormous amount of energy that had been released from the bodies of those fallen soldiers in a very short period of time. Could the site of such overwhelming carnage still retain much of that energy more than a century later? If so, this could help to explain the hundreds of ghost sightings reported by those who have visited the battlefields at Gettysburg, many of whom had never had a paranormal experience before or since.

Parapsychologists have separated ghost sightings into three basic categories. The first, and possibly the most infrequent, involves encounters with apparitions. An apparition is a spirit that appears to seek out human contact, showing him or herself in physical form and attempting to communicate with the living person. The second category is that of hauntings. These spirits tend to be associated with a certain place and appear to be oblivious to others around them. They may be observed by a number of different people over a period of time, and always seem to be engaged in a repetitious activity, such as walking through a room or gliding up and down a staircase. The third and probably most lively type of spirit is the poltergeist. Poltergeists are known primarily for their ability to move or levitate objects and generally create a disturbance in the building they occupy. But regardless of which category a ghost sighting falls into, the experience of seeing or "feeling" a ghostly presence can be terrifying, as you will discover when you read these pages and meet the ordinary people who have had extraordinary encounters with the unknown.

Many of my friends and acquaintances were surprised when they learned I was writing this book. "Why do you want to write a book about ghosts?" one of them asked. "I mean, you're so...normal!"

"Normal" people simply are not expected to believe in ghosts. Yet, nearly every person I spoke to during the course of researching this book had a story to tell me, or knew someone who did. In fact, it turns out that I am one of the few people involved in this project who has never had some type of paranormal experience. Have I ever seen a ghost? Nope. Do I ever want to? Not really. Do I believe ghosts exist? Absolutely.

It seems logical, given the number of ordinary folks who have reported unexplained phenomena, that there is "something" out there, something that will probably be clearly understood at some point in the future. After all, our world is teeming with invisible forces that our ancestors could not even imagine (television and radio signals, microwaves, not to mention the billions of microbes that surround and penetrate us on a daily basis). Perhaps the day will come when supernatural experiences will no longer be feared, but accepted as just another layer of our existence. But until then, settle in, turn on all the lights, and read on...

# SPIRITS OF ERIE COUNTY

To understand the origin of the spirits that inhabit Erie County, it may help to point out some of the historical events that shaped this remarkable area into what it is today.

Erie County, which of course was named after Lake Erie (which was named after the Erie Indians), was officially organized in 1803. The French had initially settled the region in the 1700's, building forts at Presque Isle and at LeBoeuf, which is now the town of Waterford. The British, then the Indians, recaptured the forts in turn before the area finally became part of the state of Pennsylvania in 1792. Even then, local Indian tribes resisted white settlement of the county. However, following "Mad" Anthony Wayne's victory over the Indians in nearby Ohio, the resulting treaty encouraged more whites to move into the area and settlement began in earnest.

Some of the folks who have told me their ghost stories have mentioned half-jokingly that "my house must be built on an Indian burial ground." As it happens, they may be right. At one point, five major Indian trails ran through various parts of Erie County, including the areas that are now Waterford, Mill Village, Corry, Albion, and the city of Erie itself.

Later, Oliver Hazard Perry defeated the British in the Battle of Lake Erie during the War of 1812, giving the United States control of the Great Lakes.

Because of its proximity to Lake Erie, certain portions of Erie County were active "stations" on the Underground Railroad. During the first half of the 19th century, large numbers of runaway slaves found their way north to freedom by passing through the towns and trails of Erie County. The Erie Canal Extension, as well as providing a main shipping and transportation route from the Ohio River to the Great Lakes, may also have been used to help these African-Americans safely reach their destinations.

Today, thousands of visitors travel to Erie County every year to enjoy Presque Isle State Park as well as the multitude of other tourist attractions and historical sites in the surrounding area. As a region steeped in wartime history and haunted by the countless human dramas that have played out here over the past two centuries, it's no wonder that Erie County is home to so many ghost stories, legends and folktales. Don't worry, though, if you decide to vacation in Erie County, chances are the spirits will keep themselves out of sight. But then again, I can't make any promises!

# MARINER MIKE

When Sam Chaffee moved from southern Pennsylvania into the small brick home in Erie he now occupies, he had no idea his new residence had a "history." The house was just the right size for a young bachelor, and was conveniently located close to what was soon to be Sam's successful business on one of Erie's main thoroughfares. However, even as his belongings were being moved into the house, Sam began to suspect that there might be something strange about his new home.

Sam told me his story on a bright Saturday afternoon in January. Before we began, Sam made it clear that he has no belief or even a particular interest in the paranormal. "I really don't even know if this stuff is real," he told me, "but so many things have happened since I moved in, I think there has to be something to it."

As we chatted at his kitchen table with the sun streaming through the window, I wondered how anything frightening could ever have occurred in this charming dwelling. Books, artwork, and nautical decorations lined the walls, while Sam's tabby cat, Izzy, purred on the windowsill.

However, as we walked through his home, Sam's description of his experiences cast the house in a very different light. An upstairs room has a door that opens and closes by itself. Cold drafts unexpectedly sweep through the living room even though all of the doors and windows are tightly closed. Splashing water is heard in the bathroom when nobody is in there. Loud music from an unknown source plays downstairs in the middle of the night.

"Everything started the day my brother, Bob, was helping me move in," Sam began. "Bob was alone in the house upstairs when he heard a crash in the kitchen. When he came downstairs, a lamp that was on the kitchen table had been smashed against the wall. When Bob went over to pick up the pieces, he saw a figure dressed all in black standing in the kitchen doorway, and then suddenly there was nobody there. He waited outside until I got back!"

"The first odd thing that I noticed myself," Sam said, "was the 'dragging' sounds. Every night at 4:00AM for almost two weeks I would wake up hearing the sound of something dragging across the floor. Izzy heard it, too, because she would be looking in the same direction. After a while it just stopped, but then the music started."

Sam went on to explain that for several nights both he and his girlfriend had heard music ("loud enough that I put a pillow over my head") coming from the downstairs living room. At first they thought the sound was from a car radio on the street, but upon looking out the window there was no car there, and when they came downstairs the music stopped.

Some of the most startling events have occurred in a small upstairs bedroom that Sam has dubbed "the creepy room." The room (which now stands empty as Sam prefers to avoid it) is very small, with one window, enough floor space for a twin bed, and a door leading to the hallway that stubbornly refuses to stay closed. Sam described what happened when he came home very late one night and decided to go into the room "just to see what would happen." As he approached the doorway, Sam says he felt "an unbelievable rush of...I don't know what. It wasn't cold air, but every hair stood up on my body." The next day, Sam talked his friend Jake into entering "the creepy room" to see if he, too, would experience the strange sensation. Jake was reluctant but finally agreed, on the condition that he could turn the light on first. "Jake walked into the room, turned the light on, and the light bulb exploded," Sam recalls. "He ran down the stairs and never went back."

Although long stretches of time go by when nothing unusual happens in the house, Sam reported that the disturbances will suddenly start up again for no apparent reason. "Just about a month ago, my girlfriend and I woke up hearing what sounded like the garbage can lids banging outside," he said. When they got up to check, the lids were securely on the cans and the sound had stopped.

Jim Kincaid, an acquaintance of Sam's who is also the previous owner of the house, confirmed one of the most interesting stories Sam told me. Jim prefaced his tale by telling me that "nothing much really happened" in the house while he and his family resided there. However, there was one thing that Jim just could not explain.

*Sam's "creepy room"*

"When my wife and I bought the house," Jim began, "there was a shoe rack hanging on the door of what Sam calls 'the creepy room.' Inside one of the pockets was a small cloth doll with a plastic head, maybe six or eight inches tall. I threw it away, but two or three days later it turned up in the bedroom. I threw it away again. A day or two later, it was back. This time, I thought maybe my wife liked it and had taken it out of the garbage, but she didn't know anything about it. So I threw it away a third time, and sure enough it showed up again. At that point I just figured it was supposed to stay. I didn't think much of it at the time, just chalked it up to weirdness. Later, when we added a room onto the house,

15

I sealed the doll into the wall and that was the end of it."

According to Sam, though, that wasn't the end of it. Just two nights before our interview, Sam said a loud pounding awakened him in the middle of the night in his bedroom wall, exactly over the spot where Jim told him he had "buried" the doll years ago.

Sam's house, built in 1939, was originally owned by Michael Marin, a seaman who moved to Erie after a stint in the U.S. Navy in World War II. "Mariner Mike," as he was more commonly known, owned and operated a successful restaurant in the Erie area for most of his adult life. Vestiges of Mike's seafaring days still remain in his former home, from the anchor-shaped doorknocker on the front entrance to the basement walls reportedly built with beams from a ship's hull.

The question is, could "Mariner Mike" still be there as well? If so, why would the current occupant of the house experience so many disturbances while the previous tenants did not? According to Jim Kincaid, Sam's brother, Bob, has a theory about that.

"Mike was a family man and so was I," Jim says. "Bob thinks maybe Mike's just not happy about a bachelor living in his house."

So who knows? Maybe a couple of toddlers will make the house more tranquil?

*The house built by "Mariner Mike"*

# GUDGEONVILLE

Just a few miles south of Girard Borough, one of Pennsylvania's hidden treasures can be found in the form of a quaint covered bridge that crosses Elk Creek in Girard Township.

The bridge, built in 1868, is commonly known as Gudgeonville Bridge and lies in a densely wooded area known to the locals simply as Gudgeonville. It is speculated that the name "Gudgeonville" originated from the word "gudgeon," a wooden wagon part that was possibly manufactured here in days of old. Most of those folks living near or traveling through Gudgeonville, though, couldn't care less how the place was named. They are much more concerned with getting across the bridge without encountering a filmy apparition, or noises that literally "go bump in the night."

Over the years, a multitude of unexplained occurrences have been reported in Gudgeonville, several of them involving those who have heard the sound of horses' hooves pounding over the antique bridge in the dead of night, only to fade away after a few seconds. Bonnie DuMars is one such individual.

Bonnie recalls a night in 1965 when she and her husband, along with Bonnie's sister and her boyfriend, had a startling experience. "We were parked under the bridge," Bonnie remembers, "when all of a sudden we heard this loud clumping sound, like a bunch of horses running over the rocks. We got out of the car and searched all around with flashlights, but there was nothing there."

*Gudgeonville Bridge, Girard Township*

Another former resident of Gudgeonville is Neva Kaputa, who tells of a strikingly similar experience. Around midnight one evening in 1976, Neva was driving home alone after working the late shift at a local nursing home. As her car approached the bridge, Neva heard the unmistakable clip-clop of hooves on the wooden planks. For an instant, she also saw what looked like the outline of a horse crossing the bridge. Thinking it was strange for a horse to be running loose this late at night, Neva quickly turned her car around and went back to look again, but whatever she had seen had vanished.

A year earlier, Neva had had another bizarre

experience on the bridge. That time, though, there was no thundering of hooves, only an eerie silence. Again, Neva was returning home late after working the evening shift. The night was foggy, forcing her to drive more slowly than usual. As she carefully maneuvered her vehicle onto the narrow bridge, Neva was stunned to see the shadowy figure of a young woman suddenly appear in front of her car. The woman was holding a small child in her arms and seemed intent on tossing the child into the icy creek below. When Neva slammed on her brakes, the apparition disappeared as quickly as it had come.

Legends about the area have sprung up over the years in an attempt to explain the curious sightings. The most common tale, and the one that most Girardites will tell you, is the story of a mule allegedly killed by his drunken owner on the bridge. The unfortunate animal supposedly now haunts the creek bed and is responsible for the ghostly hoof beats heard by those who dare to venture across in the dark.

In addition to the legend of the mule, real-life tragedy has contributed to reports of supernatural happenings in Gudgeonville. "Devil's Backbone", as it is known, is a sheer cliff composed of a silt-like material that flanks the Gudgeonville Bridge on one side. At least two children have reportedly fallen to their deaths while playing on the cliff, resulting in rumors of ghostly screams being heard by travelers passing through the area.

Truth or fiction? Hard to say. Some of the tales are likely just that, stories exaggerated by local children to frighten their friends around the campfire, or to impress their cousins visiting from out of town. But to folks like

Bonnie Dumars and Neva Kaputa, there is definitely something strange going on in Gudgeonville. All I can say is, come see for yourself...if you dare.

*Devil's Backbone*

# A UFO?  HERE?

In the summer of 1966, Presque Isle State Park in Erie, Pennsylvania became the focus of national attention when a group of tourists witnessed an event they would never forget.

It all started on the evening of July 31st, 1966, when Betty Jean Klem, then 16, and her companion, Douglas Tibbets, 18, of nearby Jamestown, New York, were enjoying a picnic on Beach Six at Presque Isle Park. Betty Jean and Douglas were accompanied by another friend, Anita Haifley, 22, her two small daughters, and 26-year old Gerald LaBelle, also from the Jamestown area.

Dusk was approaching, and the friends had decided to leave the park when they discovered that their car was stuck in the sand at the east edge of the Beach Six parking lot. Gerald offered to go for help while the others remained in the car.

At around 9:30PM, while still waiting for Gerald's return, Betty Jean saw a "metallic, sort of silvery" object suddenly appear in the night sky.  The mushroom-shaped object had lights on the back of it, she reported. It approached from the north and hovered for a time, a beam of light streaming from it before it finally touched down between two trees approximately 300 yards from the car. Later, Betty Jean would give the following description to police:

*"We were sitting in the car waiting for help. We saw a star move. It got brighter. It would move fast, then dim. It came straight down. The car vibrated. I know we saw it. We had taken a walk up in that area earlier. There was nothing between those trees then. All of a sudden it was just there. It lit up the whole woods in its path. It wasn't like a searchlight. There was light along the ground, along its whole path."*

Shortly after the object landed, two park patrolmen, Ralph E. Clark and Robert Loeb, Jr., arrived on the scene to help Betty Jean and her friends get their car out of the sand. The light from the object disappeared with the arrival of the police car, Betty Jean said, and the object flew away toward the north "at a tremendous rate of speed." Neither officer saw the craft, but they did agree to search the area pointed out by Betty Jean as the landing site. Douglas went along with the officers while Betty Jean, Anita, and the children remained in the car.

While the men were gone, another event occurred that would throw Betty Jean into what police described as a "state of hysteria." Still shaken from the earlier incident, Betty Jean was sure she now saw some kind of animal near the vehicle. The creature was about six feet tall, dark in color, and stood upright like a gorilla, she said. After Betty Jean sounded the car horn, the creature moved slowly off into the bushes.

After hearing the horn, Douglas and the two officers quickly returned to the car but saw nothing. Gerald also returned a short time later and but reported seeing nothing out of the ordinary. However, an examination of the car revealed scratches that the

Jamestown visitors said were not there earlier, and the next morning police made another startling discovery.

Unusual footprints were found in the sand, some which led directly to the spot where the visitors' car had been stuck. Some of the marking on the prints appeared to have been made by claws, one officer said. Other, cone-shaped markings were found in six to eight foot intervals, leading almost in a straight line to where the car had been parked the night before and where Betty Jean insists she saw the strange creature.

Some doubted the Jamestown girl's story, believing the frightened teen probably saw a raccoon or some other animal. Dan Dascanio, police chief at Presque Isle at the time, disagreed. "I discount that," he was quoted as saying. "There are no bears out here. I don't know what it was."

A number of other unusual markings in the sand were found at Beach Six the morning after the incident. Two diamond-shaped impressions were discovered by police about 350 to 400 yards from where the car had been parked. The impressions were 18 inches wide and six to eight inches deep, about 10 to 12 feet apart. Nearby, three more impressions of an indefinite shape were found in a triangular pattern, again about 10 to 12 feet apart.

It was these mysterious markings, along with the Jamestown visitors' eyewitness accounts, that prompted Chief Dascanio to contact Wright-Patterson Air Force base in Dayton, Ohio, for help in the investigation. Major William S. Hall, an Air Force investigator, arrived at the site the day after the strange events had occurred.

Major Hall, who took plaster casts of the sand

*The parking lot at Beach 6, Presque Isle*

impressions for further study, indicated that the test results could only be released by the Secretary of the Air Force, and only if they could be explained as natural phenomena.

Meanwhile, park police were kept busy with the swarm of visitors who arrived at Presque Isle in the days that followed, attempting to get a glimpse of the area where the sighting occurred. Police also received multiple calls from Erie residents who said they, too, had seen something strange that night.

According to an article in the Erie Times-News, at least eight other individuals reported seeing an unidentified object in the sky over Presque Isle between the hours of 8:00PM and midnight on July 31st, the same time that Betty Jean and her companions reported their terrifying experience on the beach. Four of these individuals, young girls having a backyard sleepover, said they spotted the object which they described as "round and silvery", about 11:00PM that night. At first the object appeared to be a star, one girl said, but it "kept fading on and off...it was very low, and we all ran and got in the station wagon and locked the doors when we saw it."

Three days later, two area police officers reported they had observed an unidentified object flying over Lake Erie near Lawrence Park, a small borough just east of the city of Erie. The two men watched the craft for about two hours, just before dawn. When daylight broke, they say, the object moved quickly to the north and vanished. Both men described the object in a similar fashion, as a bright light that was able to move at a very high rate of speed.

Despite these additional sightings, the excitement over the strange events at Presque Isle soon died down. Five days after the incident involving Betty Jean Klem, Michael E. Wargo, Superintendent of Presque Isle State Park, issued a statement declaring the park safe "for normal use." Wargo further stated that "the investigations failed to produce any proof of a UFO landing, that none was actually observed leaving the area which is about 100 yards from the Park Administration building, and Erie County Civil Defense personnel were unable to detect any radioactivity."

So what *did* Betty Jean Klem and her companions see that night, and what (or who) was responsible for the strange markings in the sand? Alien visitors? A weather balloon? Low-flying aircraft? Bigfoot?

I guess we'll just call it another Erie County mystery.

*Beach 6, Presque Isle State Park*

# THE STERRETTANIA  MONSTER

When Dave Peters heard I was writing this book, he agreed to tell me his story even though he's a bit embarrassed by the whole thing. I've known Dave for years, and he's one of the last people I would expect to have had an out-of-the-ordinary experience. He's a quiet, down-to-earth guy with a family, a responsible job, and no interest whatsoever in supernatural happenings. Yet, he still remembers something unexplainable that happened to him on a deserted country road over twenty years ago.

It was an afternoon in late October. Dave and his friend Jake had been hunting near Sterrettania, a heavily wooded area located between Girard, Fairview and Millcreek in western Erie County. Dusk was approaching when Dave and Jake decided to head for home. The two were bouncing along in Dave's truck, chatting about the day's events, when what they saw suddenly shocked them into silence.

Standing at the edge of the road near one of Sterrettania Road's hairpin turns was what Dave can only describe as a "creature." The figure was about six feet tall, covered from head to toe with ragged dark fur. Although it appeared to have four appendages, the creature stood upright, turning its head slowly as it watched Dave and Jake drive past. The most terrifying feature, Dave recalls, was its teeth. "It had huge, long teeth," he says, "like something you would see in a horror movie."

Dave and Jake continued driving and didn't look back. In fact, the two never even discussed what they had seen until years later. Dave, an avid hunter all his life, thought he had seen every animal there was to see in the forests of Erie County. "To this day, we still don't know what it was. And just so you know," he adds jokingly, "we hadn't been drinking that day either!"

Although Dave was not aware of this at the time, the description of the creature he and Jake encountered bears striking similarities to the figure Betty Jean Klem reported seeing at Presque Isle State Park nearly ten years earlier. In fact, driving north a few miles on Sterrettania Road will take you directly into Presque Isle State Park. Hmmm....does Erie County have its very own "Bigfoot?"

# HARRIET'S GHOST

Over the past 75 years, a host of recreational areas and subdivisions have been developed along the beautiful shores of Lake Erie. Once such neighborhood, located just west of the Erie International Airport near Route 5, is apparently home to a specter whom the residents there simply refer to as "Harriet's ghost."

According to Mike Gallagher, the house he currently occupies in this lovely lakeshore community has been haunted by "Harriet's ghost" for at least fifty years.

Mike knew nothing of the ghost when he and his wife first moved into the neighborhood. After they had a child, though, the story surfaced as a result of some unusual behavior by a local babysitter. One night, when Mike and his wife returned home from an evening out, they found that all of the lights in the house had been turned on. The babysitter would not explain why, however Mike later learned that the sitter had been afraid of seeing "Harriet's ghost."

Mike's house, he explained, was built in 1880 and was originally home to a large farm family. The house was remodeled in the 1950's at the same time the farmland was converted to individual lots for the subdivision that exists today.

Harriet Austin and her family moved into what is

now Mike's house shortly after the remodeling was complete. Almost immediately, Harriet began to see a ghostly apparition in one of the second floor bedrooms, a figure that appeared as a woman clad in a long white dress. Over the years, the ghost showed herself to Harriet so frequently that Harriet often spoke to her, wondering why the spirit seemed unable to free herself from her attachment to the house.

Mike offers a theory, one he believes Harriet ascribed to as well. On the north side of the house was a well once used as a water supply for the farm family. Reportedly, a young child toppled into the well and was drowned in a tragic accident many years before Harriet and her family moved in. Concealed by an addition to the house during its renovation, the well is no longer used. Harriet believed that the woman she saw haunting the upstairs bedroom may be tied to the house on an endless search for the child lost in the well.

Even though there have been no reported sightings of "Harriet's ghost" since Harriet's death several years ago, Mike Gallagher admits he can still "feel something," including unexplained "cold spots" in the bedroom on the second floor. Perhaps "Harriet's ghost" is still around, but is now just a little choosier about who gets to see her!

# FEAR OF FLYING

When Kathy Winters agreed to share her story with me, she said that very few people knew about it because, well, "most people don't believe this kind of thing."

Kathy went on to explain how her boyfriend of 23 years had collapsed and died suddenly, and even though his death occurred five years ago, "I still miss him every day."

Kathy and her boyfriend were inseparable. The two frequently traveled together, and Bill was even with Kathy when she took her first plane ride.

Some months after Bill's death, Kathy had planned to take a trip to the west coast to visit with family. She had never flown without Bill, though, and the prospect of taking the trip alone frightened her.

"I was lying in bed the night before the trip," Kathy recalls, "feeling kind of down and worried, when all of a sudden I felt the bed move, like someone was sitting down next to me." Kathy looked, but nobody was there. "I laid down on my side, and then I felt something, a form, lying alongside me. I knew it was Bill."

Kathy said she felt no fear at the time, and immediately fell asleep. The next morning she got on the plane feeling calm and relaxed, and took the long plane trip without a hint of anxiety.

These days Kathy no longer fears traveling alone, something she definitely attributes to her longtime companion. "Bill came when I needed him."

# MORE UFOs

*"I've never really told too many people about this..."*

So begins Bev McCurdy's story. Like many people, Bev had always been hesitant about discussing her UFO sighting with anyone. In fact, even though there were several other eyewitnesses to the incident, none of them ever spoke to each other about the strange aircraft that appeared in the sky over Erie more than a decade ago.

It was a crisp fall evening in 1989. Bev and her son Bradley, then 13, were driving to the post office on Erie's east side when Bradley saw an unusual light in the distant sky.

"It was way in the distance," Bradley said, "then it straightened right out in front of us and started to come toward us, lowering at the same time. We thought it was a little airplane going to make an emergency landing right on the road."

Bev remembers there was a car behind them and two more coming toward them at the time. "Everyone stopped ...it was that close," she said.

"It went real slow, " Bradley continued. "The next

thing you know there was just a big white floodlight almost directly on top of us but over to the left a little. It was about 30 feet in the air. You could see the outline; the big white floodlight in the middle, and then three tiny little red lights in a triangle form along the edge."

Bev agreed. "It was shaped like a small stealth or something."

The craft hovered above the telephone poles for a few seconds. The man in front of Bev and Bradley's car had stepped out of his vehicle and Bev rolled down her window.

"What is it?" she yelled to the man.

"As soon as she yelled that," Bradley recalls, "all I heard was a 'whoosh' and it took off. No engine sound, nothing."

"That's all there was," Bev said. "There was no motor sound, just wind. It was gone and we couldn't see anything else. No lights in the sky, nothing."

"We left and didn't even talk to the other people," Bradley said.

"That's right," Bev remembers. "Nobody talked to anyone. It was just so strange. I think maybe all of us thought the same thing...that nobody would believe us. Afterward we never saw anything about it on television, nothing in the newspaper. It was all very frightening. Bradley and I both decided not to tell anyone about it because we figured they would think we were crazy. But we did see it, God as our witness."

# THE CHAPEL GHOST

Even though most of us think of hospitals as the place we go to feel better, we all know that sometimes quite the opposite is true. Naturally, being a patient is tremendously stressful, but for some, even visiting a hospitalized friend or relative can be an emotionally draining experience, particularly if the loved one is in danger of dying. For this reason, the hospital chapel is often a welcome respite for those seeking solace, renewed strength, or just a break from the pressure of spending long hours with a critically ill individual.

This story, which I'm told took place in an Erie County hospital, is just one of what I'm sure are many tales of miraculous events that have occurred in medical settings, a testimony to what is possible even in the midst of sorrow and death.

On a sunny spring day in 1998, Joyce Goodwin was visiting the hospital chapel to pray for her son, Joe. Joe had been ill off and on for many years, suffering from a chronic kidney disease. Although Joe had "bounced back" from medical setbacks time after time, Joyce feared that this hospitalization would be the last one. All of the traditional treatments had failed so far, and Joyce noticed that even Joe's persistently positive attitude was beginning to fade.

As she slid into a pew toward the front of the quiet

church, Joyce was glad the room was empty. It would be a relief to be alone for awhile, she thought, far from the hustle and bustle of the busy nephrology floor. Joyce's sister, Ruth, had come with her today, but understood Joyce's need for privacy. I'll just grab a bite in the cafeteria, she had said, then left Joyce alone with her thoughts.

Deep in prayer, Joyce didn't know how much time had passed when she suddenly felt a hand touch her shoulder. She looked up, assuming it was Ruth coming back from the cafeteria. Instead of her sister's face, though, Joyce saw a stately older woman with white hair smiling down at her.

"He'll be all right, " the woman said, patting Joyce's shoulder. "Everything will be fine."

Touched by the woman's sympathetic manner, Joyce abruptly burst into tears. Immediately embarrassed by her outburst in front of a stranger, Joyce looked down at the floor and tried to regain her composure. When the tears had stopped, Joyce lifted her head to apologize to the kindly woman, but to her surprise the chapel was empty.

Puzzled, Joyce got up and headed for the chapel door, thinking the woman must be just outside. On her way out she literally bumped into Ruth, who had been coming in to join her.

"Did you see that woman who just left?" Joyce asked. "You must have passed her on your way in."

"I didn't see anyone," Ruth answered. "I don't even remember seeing anybody in the hall on my way down here."

"That's strange," Joyce thought out loud. "How

could she have disappeared so fast?"

"What did she look like?" Ruth asked.

"She was sort of elderly, with white hair...." Joyce's voice trailed off as her eye caught a portrait hanging just inside the chapel door. The painting was of a lovely white-haired woman with a benevolent smile.

"That's her," Joyce said, astonished. "I'm sure that's the lady I saw. She must work here."

"Not likely," Ruth said, peering at the nameplate beneath the portrait. "According to this she donated the money to build this chapel, but she died twenty years ago."

Whoever she was, the mysterious woman's prediction came true. Within two days of Joyce's encounter in the chapel, Joe's condition began to slowly improve and he was able to leave the hospital once again.

Despite evidence to the contrary, Joyce is convinced that the woman in the portrait is the same one who spoke to her in the chapel that day, and gave her hope when she needed it most.

# THE DIAMOND MINER

Albion, Pennsylvania is a tiny community nestled in the northwest corner of the state, just along the Ohio border. The people of Albion are well known in Erie County for their resilience and courage, having recently rebuilt their town after a tornado nearly destroyed it in the spring of 1985.

The Wilson house, a stately two-story home that for decades stood proudly on Albion's main thoroughfare, was one of the historic buildings unfortunately demolished by the storm. As long as the house was standing, though, the ghost of its former owner apparently refused to part with it.

The Wilsons were an extremely wealthy couple. Mr. Wilson had been a diamond miner who made frequent trips to Africa and, like a good husband, regularly brought a supply of the precious jewels home to his wife. As she was something of a recluse and perhaps a bit eccentric as well, Mrs.Wilson reportedly hoarded the diamonds by concealing them in the backs of the paintings that adorned her walls. However, as it turned out, the sparkling stones were not the only things Mrs.Wilson kept out of sight.

Alida Polk moved into the Wilson house with her family in 1962, long after the former owners had passed away. Although Alida was only seven years old at the time, she still recalls in vivid detail what happened in her childhood bedroom, beginning shortly after she and her family had settled into their new home.

As might be expected for a young child sleeping alone in an unfamiliar bedroom, Alida woke frequently throughout the night. Each time she opened her eyes, though, Alida noticed that she wasn't alone after all. Standing at the foot of her bed was an elderly gentleman dressed in pajamas, silently watching her. Too terrified to get out of bed and run to her parent's room, Alida threw the covers over her head and waited for the man to leave. Occasionally she would peek out from under the blankets only to find him still there, staring at her wordlessly.

Alida estimates these nightly visitations went on for almost a full year. Although she tried to explain to her parents, her story was dismissed as a child's nightmare, easily understandable as part of adjusting to a new home.

"The house is locked," they would tell her, shaking their heads. "How could an old man be getting into your room every night?"

Finally, though, exasperated by her continued complaints about the strange man, Alida's parents agreed to let her try a different bedroom. After the move to her new room, Alida never saw the man again.

It was not until years later that Alida discovered a possible explanation for the apparition's persistent appearances. According to local rumor, when former owner Mr. Wilson died, his aged wife was unable to deal with the loss. For nearly three years, Mrs. Wilson had kept her deceased husband hidden in their huge empty house. His decomposed body was eventually found in the room where he had died, the same room where Alida Polk had repeatedly seen an old gentleman in pajamas at the foot of her bed.

Was Mr. Wilson trying to reclaim the bed he believed was rightfully his? And now that the house is gone, what's become of Mr. Wilson's ghost?

# MOTHERS

Several of the stories I came across while researching this book had to do, in one way or another, with the relationship between mothers and daughters. It would seem that many mothers tend to maintain an active interest in the welfare of their children even after they have passed on to the next life, evidenced by the following tales of maternal devotion.

Helen Gorny had been a self-professed skeptic of paranormal phenomena, until as she says, "it happened to me." Helen, at the age of twenty and newly married, had taken on the daunting task of caring for her terminally ill, single mother while at the same time helping to raise her younger sister, Mary, who was ten years old at the time.

After her mother's death, Helen brought her sister home to live with her. One night shortly thereafter, Helen was in bed asleep when she suddenly woke with a start, sure she had heard her mother's voice whispering in her ear.

"Dolly...Dolly...I can't find your sister," the voice said urgently. Helen, who had been nicknamed "Dolly" as a child, looked up to see her mother standing next to the bed.

"Dolly..." her mother said anxiously. "I can't find Mary."

Helen remembers the decades-old incident "just as clearly as if it happened last night," she recalls. "I didn't feel afraid at all. I got out of bed and took my mother to Mary's room. I told her that Mary lives with me now. After that, she just faded away and I never saw her again."

Helen tells of another mother-daughter tale she and several others experienced while working the night shift at a local hospital.

A young woman was brought in suffering severe head injuries from a car accident that also had killed her small daughter. The woman was in a coma for an extended period of time, kept alive by a feeding tube and other life-support equipment. Her bed was positioned next to the window on one of the upper floors of the facility. On several occasions, nurses caring for the young woman would enter the room and see the specter of a little girl sitting on the ledge outside the window, peering in at the woman in the bed.

Apparently the child was waiting for her mother to join her, because after the woman's death the little girl's regular appearances ceased.

My Aunt Hattie used to tell her own mother-related ghost story quite frequently when I was growing up. Aunt Hattie lived in a huge old Victorian house just a few blocks away from my childhood home. Although Aunt Hattie was a wonderful woman, none of us cared to spend the night at her house as children, or even stay inside the house for very long in the daytime.

Even though she lived alone and the house had a number of comfortable bedrooms, Aunt Hattie always preferred to sleep in the attic room. Her mother had died when Hattie was quite young, and Aunt Hattie insisted that an apparition of her mother would often appear to her and try to sit on the end of her bed, but only when she slept in the attic room. Although the ghostly woman never spoke, I believe Aunt Hattie just liked the feeling of being close to the woman she was never able to know in life.

# MURDER IN A SMALL TOWN

Much of western Erie County consists of wide-open countryside, filled with cornfields and narrow winding back roads leading to isolated farmhouses. One such farmhouse, located just outside the small town of Girard, was the scene of a grisly double murder in 1933. In the decades since then, rumors have run rampant in the Girard area that the house is haunted, and the present owners of the century-old farmhouse don't disagree.

Don "Buzz" Green and his family have lived in the farmhouse since the 1960s. Buzz believes the spirit of one of the murdered individuals remains in the house, something he and his family have simply accepted as a fact of life.

"We think Miss Biegert is still here," Buzz says.

Johanna Biegert and her brother Albert had lived together in what is now the Green farmhouse their entire lives. The Biegerts were reportedly somewhat reclusive and rarely, if ever, left their farm. The story of their brutal murder and the subsequent investigation is almost as bizarre as some of the apparently supernatural occurrences that have taken place in the house since then.

On August 4, 1933, a local veterinarian who had come to the farm to check the cattle for tuberculosis discovered the bodies of Johanna Biegert, 70, and her brother Albert, 72. Miss Biegert, who had been severely beaten, was found dead on the kitchen floor of the house. Albert was in the barn, and despite having been stabbed numerous times with a pitchfork, was still alive. Albert was taken to an Erie hospital where he died the next day, having been unable to identify his attacker.

Police believed the motive for the killings was robbery, as the Biegerts were thought to have been suspicious of banks and therefore kept a sizable sum of money in their home. The house had been ransacked when police arrived, and less than thirty dollars was found.

The murders set off a lengthy investigation that kept the usually quiet town of Girard buzzing for weeks. County Detective Leroy Search and Constable J. O. Badders set up a headquarters in the borough hall where more than one hundred individuals, including a nephew of the victims, were questioned about the Biegerts and the circumstances surrounding their deaths.

Wild rumors and speculation about who was responsible for the heinous act spread throughout Girard and the surrounding area. My father, who had lived across the road from the elderly siblings as a child and had regularly received milk and cookies from the doting Miss Biegert, passed one of the more popular rumors on to me. The Biegerts had kept a talking parrot in a cage in their parlor, he told me, and after the murders the parrot persistently screeched to police, "The bald man did it! The bald man did it!"

In another pet-related report (this one confirmed by newspaper accounts), a startling act by the Biegert's nephew generated suspicion that he may have somehow been involved in the killings. The Biegert's hound dog, said to have been found locked in one of the rooms after the murders, was shot to death by the couple's nephew a few days after the killings, supposedly for failure to do his duty as a watchdog. Deputy Sheriff Walter Smoot criticized the act.

"The dog might have been able to help us a lot," Smoot was quoted as saying. "I'll bet money that if we suspected a man of the killing, the dog would have recognized him. I can't see any reason why that dog was killed."

All speculation was finally laid aside in late September, when more than six weeks after the crime, a 26-year-old illiterate farmhand was arrested and charged with the murders. The suspect, Thomas Smith, was being held by police in nearby Wesleyville due to a minor dispute with another man over ownership of a car. During questioning, Smith accidentally mentioned the name "Lynn Sloan," an acquaintance of his who, coincidentally, had been under surveillance in connection with the Biegert murders. In the somewhat-less-than-objective writing style of the era, a headline in the Erie Times News dated September 30, 1933, revealed a strange twist to the story:

"Fiendish Murderer Also Admits Plot To Kill Third Victim...Thomas E. Smith, 26, Tells of Gruesome Slaughter of Aged Biegerts in Farm Home on Aug. 4; Implicates Half-Breed Indian; Reveals Plan to Bash in Brains of Girard Farmer So Man's Wife Could Collect $8,000 Insurance, Wed His Accomplice."

Six years earlier, Thomas Smith had briefly met the elderly Biegerts while working as a hired hand on a Girard farm owned by George Luther and his wife

Hattie. As it happened, Hattie Luther had been carrying on an affair with another hired hand named Lynn Sloan, a self-described "half-breed" Indian originally from the Cornplanter Reservation in New York State.

According to newspaper accounts of the Biegert investigation, Hattie Luther, anxious to be free to marry her lover, had offered Smith and Sloan a portion of the proceeds from George Luther's $8,000 insurance policy if the two men would murder her husband. Thomas Smith initially confessed to police that he and Sloan had killed the Biegerts for their money and then had planned to kill George Luther. The following day, however, Smith declared he had given a false confession and knew nothing of either crime.

Thomas Smith continued to confound investigators by alternately confessing to, and then denying the killings. A break in the case came when police took Smith back to the Biegert farm for further questioning. Almost immediately, Smith began to re-enact the murders, describing the exact position of the bodies and other details that could only be known by someone with direct knowledge of the crime. Smith again denied that he had an accomplice or a motive, stating only that he believed the devil had possessed him and caused him to commit the slayings.

In November of 1933, a grand jury freed Lynn Sloan and Hattie Luther, citing insufficient evidence of conspiracy in the alleged plot to kill George Luther. Thomas Smith (who, by the way, was *not* bald), was declared insane and was permanently committed to the Fairview Hospital for the Criminally Insane near Philadelphia.

Evidently, though, Johanna Biegert was not content even after the incarceration of her confessed murderer. Buzz Green and his family have experienced a number of disturbances in their home over the years which they attribute to the spirit of Miss Biegert.

According to a 1984 article in Girard's newspaper, The Cosmopolite Herald, Buzz's wife Gina says the family has never been afraid of the ghost in their house. "There's no feeling of cold or menace or anything like that. Things have happened, things we can't explain, but she's pretty peaceful overall."

Even so, the Green's house was anything but peaceful in the early morning hours of October 31, 1977. About 3:00AM, Buzz and Gina were awakened by a noise so loud they thought at first it was either a tornado or a freight train hitting the house. The Greens watched in amazement as books hurled themselves off the shelves at the end of their bedroom, then flew *up* the staircase outside of the room. The disturbance lasted only a minute or two, and oddly enough did not awaken anyone else in the house. The Greens laughed to themselves when they realized this unnerving event had occurred on Halloween morning!

Most of the unexplained occurrences have taken place in the bedrooms of the house, particularly in an upstairs room that was once occupied by the Green daughters. A pair of lamps was frequently seen moving by themselves, and one of the daughters reported occasionally seeing a female apparition at the top of the stairs near the bedroom. The Greens also note that none of their family pets would enter the bedroom willingly, but would wait in the hall outside until their owner came out.

Could the family dogs have been "spooked" by the spirit of the Biegert's murdered pet? Or perhaps by the unfortunate lady herself? Regardless of who or what was causing the strange incidents in the Green's home, though, there has been little activity lately. Buzz believes this might be an indication that Miss Biegert's restless spirit no longer feels the need to make her presence known.

"She did most of her carousing in the bedroom upstairs, but she hasn't done much of anything for quite a while," Buzz told me. "After the girls moved out, I turned that bedroom into a 'train room' for my model trains. I think she likes the trains, because since then she hasn't done anything. I think she's probably finally at peace."

# SHEP

*The story of Shep, the graveyard dog, is not a tale of the supernatural. However, I include it here because of its significance in the local lore of western Erie County.*

For more than a century, the statue of "Shep" presided over the northeast section of the Girard Cemetery. Girard is a town filled with reminders of the past. From the Civil War monument that bisects Main Street to the cast iron deer, lions, and cannons that adorn the town square, remnants of Girard's rich history are everywhere. None of these landmarks, though, have held more fascination for Girardites over the years than the statue of Shep.

Nearly everyone in town has a story about the dog who inspired the statue. The most popular legend is that Shep had refused to eat after the death of his master and was eventually buried in the plot alongside him. Others believe the dog was euthanized at his master's request upon his death, again so they could be buried together.

The actual story, however, is considerably less romantic. The unfortunate Shep was poisoned several years after his master's death in 1881 and was buried on the family's property in nearby Miles Grove, now Lake

City, Pennsylvania.

Mrs. H.C. Davis, widow of the dog's owner, commissioned the statue of Shep in 1889. A photograph was used to sculpt the cast zinc figure of a life-size Shep sitting in a captain's chair, tail curled around his feet. The sculpture was placed in Girard Cemetery to mark the Davis family plot, and there it remained, sparking the imaginations of generations of townspeople for more than one hundred years.

Then, on September 30, 1993, Shep suddenly disappeared from his post, the victim of an apparent theft. The Girard community was stunned and angered by the news. Many felt it as a personal loss, a part of Girard's collective memory and heritage, now vanished.

"That statue was the one everyone looked for when they drove past the cemetery," said Donna Ahl, Girard's mayor at the time. "It's been there ever since I can remember. It was near my family's plot, and it was THE thing to show off to visitors when we were kids."

A reward fund was quickly organized, flyers bearing a photograph of the statue were distributed nationwide, and the local police began an intensive investigation into the theft. Despite these efforts, years went by without a solid lead in the case and Girard's citizens became less and less hopeful that the statue would ever be recovered.

Nearly four years to the day since Shep's disappearance, Girard police received a phone call from an antique dealer in New Haven, Connecticut. The dealer had recently purchased a statue that matched the description of Girard's missing Shep.

*Shep*
*Photo courtesy of the West County Historical*
*Association*

According to the police report, the dealer had seen one of the flyers containing Shep's photo, and was convinced that the statue he possessed was the same one that had been stolen from Girard Cemetery years before.

With the help of information obtained from the dealer, Girard police began the painstaking task of tracing Shep's journey from the date of the theft until it came into the possession of its current owner. The statue had apparently passed through a succession of antique dealers in several states, including Pennsylvania, Ohio, Maine, and Connecticut, at prices ranging from $6,000 up to the $20,000 paid by the Connecticut dealer.

Unfortunately, the search for those responsible for the theft of the dog came to a standstill when it was discovered that one of the early "owners" of the statue had died in 1995, making further investigation difficult, if not impossible.

Although apprehension of the thieves was unlikely, this hardly mattered to the jubilant Girardites once the dog was located. "Hot Dog! Statue Stolen From Cemetery Is Found!" screamed the headline of the local newspaper. The antique dealer had graciously agreed to return the statue, and a number of Girard citizens stood ready to foot the $800 bill to have Shep shipped home.

Amid the excitement of Shep's return, however, a new problem arose. Once the statue was returned to the cemetery, how could it be protected from another theft? A number of suggestions were considered by the community as well as by the family of H.C. Davis, rightful owners of the dog. A replica of the statue could be placed in the cemetery, while the original was housed at a local museum. Or, a monument company offered to affix the statue to a cement base, making it more difficult to remove from the cemetery.

In the end, a decision was reached that seemed to satisfy the majority of those involved. The statue was donated to the borough of Girard by Mr. Davis's descendants, then placed in the lobby of the town hall, just adjacent to the Police Department. Although some feel that the statue loses a bit of its charm in its current location, most agree that protecting the treasure antique is well worth it.

# THE GENERAL

If you ask the average Erieite who "Mad " Anthony Wayne was, you're likely to get a variety of answers. Most know he was a soldier, some can tell you he fought in the Revolutionary War. But the one and only thing that stands out for most of us is the story about his body being boiled in a big black kettle.

It's not our fault, really. After all, even though Wayne was an outstanding military and political figure during and after the American Revolution, the only thing he did while he was in Erie was...die.

But before we get into the strange circumstances surrounding Wayne's burial and the legendary search for his missing bones, here is a brief overview of the "mad" general's life and untimely death, for those of us who may have forgotten what we learned in school.

Anthony Wayne was born on New Year's Day, 1745, in Chester County, Pennsylvania. His grandparents had moved to America in the 1700's from Europe, where Wayne's grandfather had served in the British army. Perhaps inspired in part by his family's military history, and not willing to settle for the more routine life of a Pennsylvania farmer, Wayne joined the Continental Army when the Revolutionary War broke out in 1776.

From the start, Anthony Wayne had a reputation for being a bit wild. As a general, he preferred to fight alongside his men rather than observing from afar. His impetuous nature and seemingly reckless behavior on the battlefield soon earned him the nickname "Mad Anthony," a moniker that stuck with him throughout his career.

Despite his outward appearance, however, Wayne was actually a thoughtful and well-organized commander. Each military action was carefully planned, and Wayne paid great attention to the comfort of his men. In fact, he reportedly was something of a fashion-conscious "dandy," regularly requesting improved, more stylish uniforms as well as barber services for the men under his command.

Labeled by his detractors as a foul-mouthed braggart, Wayne was nonetheless an excellent soldier trusted by the likes of George Washington, with whom he spent the famous and deadly winter at Valley Forge. Washington respected Wayne's military prowess and frequently assigned him to difficult commands throughout their service together.

After the Revolutionary War was over, Anthony Wayne went on to victories in the conflict between the United States Army and the Native American tribes who were fighting to keep their homeland. Probably the most well known of these was the Battle of Fallen Timbers in Ohio, where Wayne's victory led the way to a significant treaty with the Native Americans and allowed for further expansion of settlers to the west.

Off the battlefield, General Wayne was known for his flamboyant personality and his taste for the company of beautiful women. Although married with two children, Margaretta and Isaac, Wayne was said to have been generally unsuccessful as a family man, spending most of his time in the pursuit of his political and military ambitions.

While stationed in Detroit in 1796, General Wayne decided to move his command east to Pittsburgh, Pennsylvania. He planned to travel by boat from Detroit to Presque Isle, Pennsylvania, then south to Pittsburgh from there. The trip was unfortunately interrupted when Wayne was bedridden with a severe case of gout, an illness from which he had suffered periodically throughout his life.

Wayne's ship made it to Presque Isle in mid-November, 1796. Very ill by this time, Wayne was moved from the boat to the Presque Isle blockhouse where he awaited the arrival of his physician who had been summoned from Detroit. However, his condition grew rapidly worse, and by the time the doctor arrived it was too late. General "Mad" Anthony Wayne died on December 15, 1796, at the age of 51.

Anthony Wayne was buried the next day beneath the flagpole near the blockhouse where he died, at what was then Fort Presque Isle. A simple stone carved with Wayne's initials was placed on the grave.

In 1809, the citizens of Chester County, seeking to honor General Wayne's memory, requested that his remains be returned for reburial in the family plot. Wayne's son, Isaac, agreed to make the trip to Erie to arrange for the exhumation of his father's body.

When Isaac arrived in Erie, he spoke with Dr. J.C. Wallace and explained what needed to be done. Dr. Wallace agreed to prepare the General's body, which he believed would be severely decomposed, for the journey back to Chester County.

Upon opening the grave, Dr. Wallace was astonished to find that very little decomposition had occurred in the thirteen years since Wayne's death. Contrary to what the doctor had previously told Isaac Wayne, transferring the body in its current state would be extremely difficult. So, the resourceful Dr. Wallace did what he felt would be most expedient under the circumstances. He placed the body in a large iron kettle and boiled it to remove the flesh from the bones. Then, using his surgical equipment, the doctor carefully scraped the remaining tissue from the bones.

After the bones were clean, Dr. Wallace returned them to Isaac, for they could now easily be transported by wagon for interment in Chester County. On October 4, 1809, following a lengthy ceremony, the bones of General Anthony Wayne were buried at St. David's Church near Waynesborough, Pennsylvania. The rest of the remains were returned to Wayne's original coffin and reburied at the blockhouse on Presque Isle.

The blockhouse burned in 1852 and a replica, now located at East 3rd and Ash Streets in Erie, was rebuilt in 1880 as a memorial to General Wayne. The original cauldron used to boil the General's body is currently on display at the Erie County Historical Society and Museums.

End of story, right?

Not so, if you believe in legends. You see, some say that while traveling the hundreds of miles of bumpy roads between Erie and Chester County, a few of Anthony Wayne's bones fell off Isaac's wagon and were lost. Always fastidious about his appearance, General Wayne certainly would not be pleased about part of his remains being scattered alongside a country road.

So as the story goes, every New Year's Day on the anniversary of his birth, the ghost of "Mad" Anthony Wayne can be seen riding the roads between Erie and Chester County on an endless search for his missing bones.

*The blockhouse on Presque Isle*

# AX MURDER HOLLOW

If you happen to be driving through Erie County on Halloween night, be careful to avoid turning down Thomas Road in Millcreek Township. This rural stretch of road, which is nearly deserted at any other time of the year, is jammed with traffic on Halloween. Cars line both sides of the road as thrill seekers search the wooded area known as "Ax Murder Hollow," anxious for a glimpse of the ghostly killer said to haunt the forest just off Thomas Road for at least 60 years.

Several versions of this local legend have been passed down over the years. The most common account involves a farmer who lived with his wife and children in an old house on the hill overlooking the hollow. One night, overcome with rage after discovering that his wife had been unfaithful, the jealous farmer chased his wife and children down the hill and through the hollow, eventually killing and dismembering the entire family with his ax. The farmer was never seen again, but his ax-wielding ghost is said to wander the hollow at night, endlessly searching for his final victim...his wife's lover. Specters of the man's wife and children have also been spotted conducting their own search of the hollow in an attempt to retrieve their missing body parts.

An alternate version of the tale has to do with a band of gypsies who were traveling through Millcreek Township when they decided to camp in the hollow for the night. During that fateful night, the leader of the clan learned that his wife had been cheating on him. Reportedly, the man immediately cut off his wife's head with an ax, then hid the head in the nearby Weis Library building located on the corner of Thomas and Sterrettania Roads.

Despite the persistent re-telling of the Ax Murder Hollow legend, no actual proof has ever been documented to substantiate these stories, no disembodied heads have been discovered in the area, and the farmhouse on the hill is no longer there. Still, many insist there is something strange about the woods along Thomas Road. A set of stone steps leading from the former house on the hill are said to be bloodstained even to this day. And if you dare to walk the path through the densely wooded hollow, some say, you will notice that one side of the path is alive with flowers and chirping birds, but the other side, the side associated with the murders, is eerily quiet and devoid of wildlife.

*Thomas Road, Millcreek Township*

Over the years, the story of Ax Murder Hollow has grown to include another tale of the "urban legend" variety. Young people who have used the hollow as a favorite parking spot give this warning to their friends: whatever you do, make sure you don't stop on the third bridge over the hollow. The road that passes through the area does indeed contain three bridges. As the story goes, no harm will befall you on the first two, but if your car should stall on the third bridge, you will never return from... Ax Murder Hollow.

# THE HAUNTED RING

The sprawling campus of Mercyhurst College is undoubtedly one of the most breathtakingly beautiful in Erie County. Founded by members of the Sisters of Mercy in the early twentieth century, the college sits atop a hill overlooking Lake Erie in the southeast portion of the city of Erie.

Driving through the main gates, one is immediately struck by the magnificent architecture of the Tudor-style buildings, interspersed with the lush greenery of well-kept lawns. Even with the throngs of chattering students busily moving between buildings on their way to classes, the halls and grounds of the college somehow manage to maintain an aura of hushed, respectful serenity.

Despite these pristine surroundings, however, Mercyhurst is reportedly home to at least three restless ghosts. One, the spirit of a former groundskeeper, was observed tending his beloved fruit trees in the apple orchard near the campus long after the death of his earthly body. The other two are said to haunt the school's exquisitely beautiful chapel.

According to the Mercyhurst alumnus who recounted these tales to me, the first ghost whose presence is said to have been felt there is that of a wealthy European benefactor who actually gifted the college with its chapel, an exact replica of one he had seen and loved in France. In fact, the gentleman was so enamored with the Mercyhurst chapel that he had fervently wished to be interred there upon his death. Unfortunately, the man was found to be involved in some less-than-legal dealings in his native country. He was tried, hung, and ultimately buried in Europe, never again to see the chapel he had hoped would be his final resting place. However, it would seem that even in death, this headstrong gentleman refused to be deterred from his goal. His presence is said to have been felt by many at the college, leading some to believe that his spirit was so attached to the Mercyhurst chapel that he traveled across time, space, and even the Atlantic Ocean to make his eternal home in Erie, Pennsylvania.

The second ghost thought to haunt the chapel is that of a young woman who attended Mercyhurst College decades ago, long before the school converted to its present "coed" status. As the story goes, the woman (who I will refer to as "Rose") was very much in love and engaged to be married to a young man from a nearby college. Their marriage plans were unfortunately postponed when war broke out and the young man was sent to fight overseas. Some months later, Rose, who had been continuing her studies at Mercyhurst, received the devastating news that her betrothed had been killed in battle.

Distraught, Rose swore that she could never love another man, and decided to dedicate the rest of her life to God by becoming a nun. One day after Rose had taken her final vows, she visited the Mercyhurst chapel. Kneeling before the statue of the Christ Child, Rose placed her engagement ring on the fingers of the baby

Jesus, a symbol of her everlasting devotion to the Church. With this gesture, Rose believed she had finally freed herself from the pain of her tragic past. Relieved, she left the chapel ready to begin her new life.

Rose remained at Mercyhurst College, finding peace and fulfillment by serving God with the Sisters of Mercy. However, her contentment was not to last.

One day shortly after the war ended, a young man arrived at the college looking for Rose, bearing what he hoped would be joyful news for her. Apparently, the reports of her fiancé's death had been erroneous. He was literally back from the dead and looking forward to a long life with the woman he loved.

Rose was beside herself. Unable to face the impossible decision of choosing between the man she loved and her vows to the Church, the heartbroken Rose hung herself in a small dormitory room just above the chapel.

Some years after Rose's death, a female student at Mercyhurst decided to play a prank on her boyfriend who was planning to visit her for the weekend. She took Rose's ring, which was still intact on the finger of the Christ Child statue, intending to wear it when her boyfriend arrived and fool him into thinking she was marrying someone else. Before he could make it to their rendezvous, however, he was involved in a freak auto accident and instantly killed.

Rumor quickly spread across the campus that Rose's ring was the cause of the poor young man's unexpected demise. To prevent the possibility of further tragedies, the ring was supposedly buried in a secret location somewhere on the college grounds. Rose's unhappy ghost is believed to still haunt the chapel, searching for the star-crossed ring she left behind those many years ago.

Truth, or fiction?  Let the reader decide.

# ACKNOWLEDGEMENTS

Writing a book such as this one is never the work of the author alone. This book would not have been possible without the support and contributions of dozens of friends, family, and acquaintances, not to mention the keepers of the sometimes very personal stories that fill these pages.

My deepest thanks to Alida Polk for her story leads as well as her ongoing interest and encouragement.

Thanks also to the West County Historical Association for the use of their files, particularly to Steve and Beth Hudson for their invaluable contribution to the story of the Biegerts.

I would also like to say a heartfelt thank you to the following individuals who all helped with this project in one way or another: Andrea and Bob Greene, Caroline Veith, Judy Pratt, Dave Shaffer, Julie Janiuk, Karen Beck, Jeff Ahl, Connie Kendra, Marcia Nitczynski, Tim Hahn of the Erie Times News, and the very knowledgeable and helpful individuals at the Erie History Center, the Cosmopolite Herald, the Albion Public Library, and the Raymond Blasco Memorial Library. Your assistance was greatly appreciated.

Particularly to all of the people who contacted me and allowed me to include your stories here, I thank you.

Finally, a special thanks to Amanda Wincik for your computer wizardry, and to Zachary Wincik for your help with the photographs. I couldn't have done it without you.

# SOURCES

## INTRODUCTION

Holzer, Hans. *Ghosts*. Black Dog & Leventhal Publishers, Inc., New York, 1997

Robinson, Lynn A., M.Ed. and Carlson-Finnerty, LaVonne. *Being Psychic*. Alpha Books, Indianapolis, IN, 1999

Nesbitt, Mark. *More Ghosts of Gettysburg*. Thomas Publications, Gettysburg, PA, 1992

## SPIRITS OF ERIE COUNTY

Swetnam, George and Smith, Helene. *A Guidebook to Historic Western Pennsylvania*. University of Pittsburgh Press, 1976

## MARINER MIKE

*Erie Times News*, February 9, 1979

Personal interview with Sam Chaffee (pseud.), January 2002

Telephone interview with Jim Kincaid (pseud.), January 2002

## GUDGEONVILLE

Local legend

Telephone interview with Neva Kaputa, January 2002

Telephone interview with Bonnie DuMars, January 2002

*The Cosmopolite Herald*, October 19, 1982

# A UFO? HERE?

*Erie Times News*, August 1, 1966
*Erie Times News*, August 2, 1966
*Erie Times News*, August 3, 1966
*Erie Times News*, August 5, 1966

# THE STERRETTANIA MONSTER

Personal interview with Dave Peters (pseud.), January 2002

# HARRIET'S GHOST

Telephone interview with Mike Gallagher, February 2002

# FEAR OF FLYING

Telephone interview with Kathy Winters (pseud.), February 2002

# MORE UFOs

Taped interview with Bev McCurdy and Bradley McCurdy, March 2002

# THE CHAPEL GHOST

Anonymous contributor

THE DIAMOND MINER

Taped interview with Alida Polk, January 2002


MOTHERS

Personal interview with Helen Gorny, February 2002
Author's personal recollection


MURDER IN A SMALL TOWN

Telephone interview with Don Green, February 2002
*Erie Times News*, August 4, 1933
*Erie Times News*, August 5, 1933
*Erie Times News*, September 19, 1933
*Erie Times News*, September 20, 1933
*Erie Times News*, October 25, 1933
*The Cosmopolite Herald*, October 31, 1984


SHEP

*The Cosmopolite Herald*, September 28, 1997
Author's personal files


THE GENERAL

Nelson, Paul David. *Anthony Wayne, Soldier of the Early Republic.*
Indiana University Press, Bloomington, 1985
*Erie Times News*, December 12, 1996

AX MURDER HOLLOW

Local legend
Dave Richards, "Erie Legends," *Erie Times News*, January 21, 2001


THE HAUNTED RING

Taped interview with anonymous source, March 2002
"Mercyhurst History," Mercyhurst College Online, 2001

# ABOUT THE AUTHOR

Stephanie Wincik is a full-time registered nurse and part-time freelance writer and history buff. She lives in Erie County with her husband and two teenage children. She is currently working on a historical novel for young adult readers.